THE GIGOLO OF THE COUNTRY PARK

by

Doris Anne Beaulieu

I dedicate this book to a lifelong friend who has been in shock many times in her life starting from childhood. She has truly lived the hard way and has overcome a lot. However, this shocker took the cake.

She's the kind of friend you would always want to go with you on a trip to guarantee a good time and also has a way with words to protect you from harm of others. She can see trouble before you get there. She's fun, honest, and straightforward. She won't tell you what you want to hear but tell you what you need to hear. As a certified trained community advocate, I bring these types of happenings in the communities to life in hopes of helping, especially seniors who are trapped within themselves, see they're not alone. They tend to keep these unfair treatments to themselves out of shame or fearing what people will think because of their age. They fear being looked at as losing it or making things up. Scammers know that and prey on them in many forms. Read this story and help seniors unite for protection in your community.

Thanks, My Friend!

CONTENTS

Chapter One:
Moving in the Trailer Park

Finding a trailer park fit for a senior of older age can be hard to accomplish, on top of one with the perfect setup to fit the needs of that senior. Jill, a seventy-year-old single woman, is looking for that perfect place to call home as she moves on to the rest of her years. She visits a real estate agency to help her in finding one. She had called in the morning and discussed her requirements in detail.

JIM: You must be Jill. You spoke with me on the phone, and I found some to show you. Do you have time now to check them out?

JILL: Yes, I do.

JIM: Just follow me.

He opens the door for Jill, and they get to the first trailer on his list; he gives her the walkthrough.

JILL: This is not for me. Not the layout I was

looking for. I do want two bedrooms, and for the privacy of my guests, I would prefer the bedrooms be on opposite ends of the trailer. I also only need one bathroom to clean and a quieter trailer park.

JIM: We have one that just came on the market this morning. Very quiet as most in the park are seniors like yourself. It's on the outskirts of town. No dogs allowed, but it still needs to be set up, so it may take a month for it to be move in ready. You'll have to take the loan for the trailer with the credit union they deal with and have five thousand for the deposit.

JILL: Let's go see it.

Jill takes notice of it not being that far from downtown Lewiston where she lived her whole life. She also takes notice of how the trailer park is set up to make every trailer seem more private and is not just a straight row with trailers on both sides of the road. That makes it look very welcoming to her. Getting out of her car, she notices how quiet it is.

JIM: Well, let's see if this is more to your liking.

Jill checks out every room and the appliances. She sees which furniture she will give to relatives who help her move and which of her old furniture she will put in the trailer.

JILL: I'll take it.

JIM: Now, this place has rules to follow and live by. Like if you get a shed to store stuff like lawnmowers and garden tools, the shed needs to be painted the exact color of your trailer. When you start the account with the credit union, they will need your finances to make sure you will be able to pay your monthly bills.

JILL: I don't have a husband. Do they handle all the setups?

JIM: There are 250 trailers in this park, so they do have a maintenance crew to handle the setup of the trailer. You will have to deal with the propane people yourself and handle the cost of that setup with them. You'll also need steps in front and in back that meet their codes and they do have those for sale at the office. Now, if you don't have any more questions for me, let's go to the office and get the ball rolling on that paperwork.

Jill is very excited when moving day comes. She has her shed, but it was unpainted at the time. Her family is moving her stuff from storage to her shed to go through and decide what she will keep and what they can have to help her move.

Jill sees a truck that says maintenance as it arrives.

JILL: You two guys here to connect things?

The older man, John, looks like he's about to retire and enjoy his life. The other, his helper, is a young man named Nel. Jill feels he must be in training to take over. As he approaches Jill with a big smile, she is taken away by his smile and bright blue eyes. She had always liked a blue-eyed man her whole life.

JOHN: Yes, ma'am, we need for you to be home before connecting to make sure it is all working good inside the trailer after we connect. Don't want a problem and want to know if we need to adjust anything.

JILL: The propane people are also on their way.

JOHN: We got your electricity going yesterday for you, so you're all set there.

She thanks them for their help and for getting her new home all set up for the work she has ahead of her in organizing her new home.

The following week, Jill notices the two maintenance men, John and Nel, trimming trees on the edge of what is her space of living yard. The young guy is playing music and singing to it with a bit of a dance to him. From behind, she gives a little giggle as she can see he has a spring of a bounce to his behind. *A bubble butt,* she tells herself, as he makes the unpacking and running from shed to house a bit more enjoyable to do. At times, she finds herself giving a little dance herself, as country music always has the right beat for her. She thinks to herself that this guy loves the oldies like her. She grew up listening to what Mom and Dad played on the old record player.

Chapter Two:
Meeting The Gigolo

Another week has passed, and Jill has been getting tired of the constant washing, moving, and organizing of her new home. Today, she is taking a very late afternoon nap when she hears a knock at her door.

NEL: Hello, ma'am; remember me? I'm Nel, the maintenance helper.

JILL: Sure, come on in.

NEL: Hope you're alright? I noticed you took a few falls last week when getting boxes into the trailer from the garage.

JILL: Too busy watching you dance instead of paying attention to my work. I heard you like the oldies from my days.

NEL: Always seems to have the right beat for dancing to me.

JILL: That it does. How can I help you today?

NEL: I'm here to give you my card and offer my services.

JILL: If I need any small stuff done, I have children I can pay to do odd jobs for me. If there's a need the park has to handle, I can just call the office.

NEL: No, ma'am, you don't understand. I provide a service your husband used to provide; I know elderly people still have needs.

Jill is shocked. Her face begins to feel a burn to the point of blocking her from hearing what she is hearing at the age of 70 from this young man.

JILL: Oh dear God, I have children older than you. Shame on you; get out of my house right now.

She is beside herself and begins to push him towards the door and slams the door behind him. As she begins to shake at such a thing, she calls her son, who advises her to call the police. Jill, however, doesn't want to start any trouble where she just moved in.

JILL: Son, they don't know me, and he is their hired help, so it would just be my word against his. He's hired help and I'm a nobody to them. I feel better just telling someone and will see what happens from here on. Okay!

The next day, Jill sees the old man in maintenance working alone. She walks to John and, in a direct, stern voice, says.

JILL: Never bring Nel around my place again if any work needs to be done.

At that point, she is shaking so badly that she just turns and walks away before John has a chance to say or ask anything.

Out of fear of Nel's return, she changed her sleep timing. She now sleeps during the day and is awake at night with lights on all night. She fills her nights with the little housework she has, goes shopping or visiting till it's not proper to do so, and returns home with all lights on.

Home alone was never part of her life like this. Loneliness brings in fear she has never felt before, and that's one reason, in today's world, she wanted to live in a trailer park with other seniors; she felt that would bring her comfort and a safer place to live.

She spends the early morning hours overthinking and finds more questions than answers to all she thinks about. *There are 250 trailers here. How many seniors are alone like me? How many took this young guy up on his offer? How much of their social security is he getting from them every month? How long has he been doing this? Does the office know what their hired help is doing? Could there be others who turned him in? Is the old maintenance guy John in on it?*

While contemplating, she receives a notice in the mail from the office of the trailer park. She wonders if it's trouble because of how she talked to the old man. Despite being afraid to open it, she gathers strength and clicks it. She breathes a sigh of relief to find out it is a notice of someone new moving into the trailer park. Feeling relieved, she asks herself, *is this how Nel knew who to approach?* It surely was not for welcome to the trailer park from people. They all seem to keep to themselves, as most seniors prefer but yet enjoy talking to other people. Jill takes notice of where this new person is moving and decides she now has a new route to leave the trailer park to go to town or visit. She wants to see if that lady named Linda will be Nel's next victim.

Chapter Three:
New Comer to the Trailer Park

Linda now has the power on in her new trailer and loves to work while listening to music. Waiting for the maintenance men to arrive and hook the water and sewer up to her trailer, she grabs boxes from her shed and returns to her house to unpack them. Then, she places the empty boxes outside. She is playing the song *Lynda* by Steve Wariner and dancing to the song, unaware the maintenance men are watching her dance through the window before they knock.

Nel likes the moves she is making and has a big smile on his face when Linda turns in her dancing and sees them. Just then, Jill drives by and hears the song Linda has been playing. Nel notices Jill driving by as they walk in the trailer. Linda turns her music off and greets them.

LINDA: I'm sorry, I didn't hear you knock.

NEL: That's a 1987 song, if I remember it correctly.

LINDA: Yes, a favorite and special song for me.

JOHN: We'll get your water first, then the sewer, and check here inside to make sure all is working with no leaks in any pipes before we leave.

LINDA: Could you make like a boxed-in around the pipe in my bedroom closet so my clothes don't hit the pipe in any way or damage any of my clothes being against it?

JOHN: Nel, after we check for leaks make sure you put that extra casing to close up that area for her.

NEL: Will do, sir.

He gives Linda a big smile.

John and Nel have everything all hooked up and look at Linda.

JOHN: Linda, Nel will finish up the small details

13

as I go fill in the paperwork of what we have done at the office.

NEL (happy to see John leave): I'll start with your closet so you can get your clothes in there instead of the sofa here.

LINDA: Go ahead. I still have unpacking to do that will go into that closet.

Nel not only boxes the pipe in but also puts in a camera hidden within the closet area.

NEL: I'm all done; you can start putting your clothes in as I check your fuse box to make sure everything is on, like the fridge, washer, and dryer.

Linda grabs a handful of clothes and heads to the bedroom as Nel sets up another camera within the area of the fuse box. She starts making her way back down the hall before Nel is done covering the camera. He hollers out to Linda to turn the dryer on to see if it's working. She backtracks and goes to turn it on. Meanwhile, he finishes his covering of the camera.

NEL: Well, I'm done here, but I'd like to come back after I clean up to see if you need anymore help and talk with you on your first day in our trailer park. Maybe talk about that song you were dancing to so gracefully.

LINDA (jokingly): Oh my, you want to be my Spider Man, and I your Wonder Woman.

NEL: Just as the song wrote it.

They both start laughing.

NEL (continues): Since you're new here, I'll pick up a little snack to welcome you in. Say about seven.

LINDA: Okay, I'll need the break by then. Sure!

Linda stops bringing in boxes at five, vacuums her new trailer, and gets things cleaned up before a relaxed night talking with Nel. Feeling a little funny, she decides to wear her Wonder Woman outfit to give Nel a good laugh. She figures he's young and will get a good laugh out of the story behind it. She always liked to spice things up, even in her 60s, to live life to the fullest.

Linda has her house in order and decides there is enough time for a good shower to get the day's work off her. She unlocks her door in case Nel shows up before she is done as she looks at him as a son, helpful and kind.

Nel hears the shower going and checks the door to see it's unlocked, so he lets himself in to set up the wine, cheese with crackers, and strawberries. He pours some wine and adds a pill to it as he also takes Viagra himself for a lasting night.

Linda walks out of the bathroom dressed in a Wonder Woman outfit from head to toe. When she sees Nel in a Spider Man outfit, they both begin to laugh.

NEL: I just had to do it after the way you were dancing today.

LINDA: I just wanted a good laugh. It's been so long since I had a good laugh. My husband and I used to play dress up for date night and that kept us young. We had to keep dreaming up new outfits and acts to go with it. I think we could have done well in the movies.

NEL: That's so cool to hear. Come sit and we can talk while having wine and cheese.

Linda takes a seat on the rocker beside the couch where Nel was sitting.

LINDA: I like red wine and this is a good year. We learned a lot about wine and used to go visit wineries around the world when he was alive and we were younger. We'd save up all year for one good trip a year. He knew how to enjoy life and I was grateful for it.

NEL: So, Linda, tell me the story as to why you like the song *Lynda* so much?

LINDA: Well, before we even started to date, I was a waitress and when I heard that song come on the jukebox, I knew he was out there. I was surely right. We began to talk and started dating. We listened to it whenever things in life got tough for us, or we were feeling down. So today, I felt like I had abandoned our old home and wanted to feel comfort. So I played it to get that feeling inside me. It made me feel alive and at peace that he understood where I was in life. I needed to downsize; the old house was just too much for me, as I didn't need that big of a place with the kids all grown and the upkeep was too much for me now that I got older and alone.

NEL: How about we get out of this outfit, put that song on, and have a nice dance for old-time sake?

LINDA: Sure!

Linda hasn't eaten all day, and as she stands up, Nel can see the pill is working. They get out of costumes, and both have shorts on with shirt-sleeve shirts. Nothing underneath. She puts the song on and they begin to dance. Nel knows where to place himself so his camera is on her to capture all her facial expressions.

NEL: What was your husband's name?

LINDA: Charlie!

NEL: Well, pretend you're dancing with Charlie one more time.

Nell begins to kiss her as his hands slowly wrap around one of her breasts. She allows it to happen with her eyes closed as he plays with the nipple to get her aroused and he feels her want for more. He slides his hand softly between her legs as he caresses her neck and she pulls him back for a kiss. He begins to tap softly on her clit at the beat of the drum in the song. He saw how she was dancing to the beat earlier during the day. She is getting very wet with lusty faces and moans are coming from her as Nel continues. She rips his shirt off and the song replays again.

Yes, keep the machine running comes on the song, and Linda repeats it as she is about to reach her climax. When she does, Nel directs her down gently to her knees and pulls his pants down as he places his penis in position to give him head. He allows her to service him in a delightful way. He then picks her up to take her to bed. He's been serviced but wants more due to the Viagra pill he took. Making sure to wear a condom as he always does and gets the lube from his pocket before taking his shorts off. The camera he placed in the bedroom would face her, not him, as he lubes her anus up slowly and softly, putting his fingers in to lube inside and stretch her out to receive him.

Nel continues to have his way with Linda as he brings his penis to her butt hole for extra self-pleasure, then coming on her face and rubbing it all over her body while her head is in direct view of the camera to capture all her facial expressions while he goes in the back door. Her moaning and groaning get loud as if this had never happened to her before. The camera captures everything. Linda passes out. Nel gets dressed, leaving his ripped t-shirt on her pillow, taking his cameras, wines, and glasses with him. He turns off the music that is repeating itself, locks the doors, and leaves.

Linda wakes in the morning with a terrible headache and passes gas like she has never done before in her life. *What a dream,* she tells herself till she sees the torn shirt on her pillow. The memories start to come back to her as she sits drinking coffee to wake herself up. *Did it, could that have really happened?* She is beside herself in shame. She sees the cheese and fruits are still there, but not the wine or glasses.

LINDA (looking up and saying loudly): Oh, Charlie, I'm sorry, I don't know what came over me.

She remembers the wine; when she had it with Charlie, it did not affect her that way. She starts believing he must have put something in it because she can only remember getting up to play that song. Nothing is clear after that, but how was Nel's shirt torn or even on her pillow in the bedroom, of all places. She spends her day with the doors locked, trying to think of what happened.

The day turns to night. The early morning sun beams down on Linda and warms her up. She decides she needs to keep unpacking and get her home in order to move forward in her life. She hears a knock on her door and peeks to see who it is to find a lady standing there. She unlocks the door to welcome the guest.

JILL: Hi I'm Jill, stopping in to welcome you to the park.

She has coffee and donuts.

JILL (continues): I noticed yesterday that boxes were still outside and wanted to see if you were alright or needed help to get them inside before the rain comes. I can help you bring the boxes in till ten then I must go to my appointment. The rain is due around noon, from what the weather man said.

The girls get going on getting all the boxes in. As they do so, they both stop when they see Nel driving by. Jill takes notice of Linda's reaction. Linda asks Jill to get the boxes in quickly before the rain. She knew from Nel's reaction that things did not go well at all. Not wanting to pry, Jill asks no questions even though Linda's reaction had said it all.

LINDA: Jill, thank you for your kindness in helping me this morning and getting these boxes in. I really appreciate it more than you know.

Jill hears the door lock as she leaves.

Right before the rain came, the old maintenance man, John, comes to clear the bushes by Linda's mailbox for the mailman. Linda sees he's alone and goes out running to him.

LINDA: You best keep your partner away from my trailer, or I'll call the cops.

Than she runs back into her trailer. John is confused as this is the second time he hears this reaction. Not sure what to do or think. When he gets back to the shop, he confronts Nel about what has been said.

NEL: You know old women are picky and only

want old men around to do the work. Maybe they have a crush on you. Really, John, do you hear any of that from the good-looking young ladies in this park?

John thinks for a minute.

JOHN: Well, no, maybe you're right, but if I hear any more of it, I'll have to report it to the office.

NEL: Well, then you handle the old ones.

Nel feels he has enough going right now, anyhow, at $50 an hour or $300 a night. He's banked a good amount in the past few years. He can afford to lay back some and look for a while or at least not pick up any more ladies.

He still needed to see if he locked in Linda, so he stops by her trailer. He knocks on her door; she opens the door, but her screen door is locked.

LINDA: I don't know what happened the other night, but if you come here again, I'm going to call the police. I think you drugged me and had your way with me.

NEL: You invited me in, remember that, girl.

LINDA: Yes, but not to drug me like you did.

NEL: Well, I'll leave you this DVD to remember the night, and you best keep your mouth shut about that night if you know what's good for you, or I'll put it all over the web for the world to see.

Nel then turns and walks away. Linda waits till she can no longer see him drive away before getting the tape from the top steps where Nel left it. She watches the DVD in total shock, shaking and crying, curled up in her bed all night. As she cries, she talks out loud to an empty room.

LINDA: How dare he do that? He's sick, a very sick man.

Seeing her own face on the tape has overtaken her with such pain. She tells herself she will never ever trust another man again. She now understands all the gas she had in the morning like she never had before in her life. She breaks the DVD into many pieces as she throws it into the trash. She takes another shower and sleeps in come morning.

Chapter Four:
Slow Hand Betty

Betty has been in the trailer park for five years now. When she notices water all over the slab that her trailer sits on, she calls the office to tell them of her problem. They tell her the maintenance men will be over after lunch and ask if she'll be home in case it's something inside the trailer and not outside. Betty assured them she would be.

NEL: I see your problem, Betty. It seems a seal has broken where the town water and the trailer connect, so I will have to turn all your water off and drain it all to put a new one in.

Betty collects the water she will need for the afternoon first and offers Nel a glass of ice tea while they let the water drain for the repairs. He always likes to eat for free and has done well in saving money that way.

NEL: Boy, that smells good; what you cooking?

BETTY (who used to work as a cook in her younger days): Betty Crocker's chicken stew. I used to be a chef and cooked all her recipes in my younger days. I always have so many leftovers. You can join me if you wish and save me from eating it all week.

Nel is slim himself with a tan to show off his muscled arms to the ladies. White tank tops are what he wears most with tight-fitted jeans to show his bubble butt. He keeps his blonde hair that has a slight wave in it just long enough for the ladies to run their hands in it, along with just enough chest hair for hand playing, too.

NEL: I can come over after work and get cleaned up, say about six.

Betty has a thing for the younger men, as a slim woman who carries her slim figure just fine, with the energy to go with it.

BETTY: Great, will see you then.

Six o'clock has arrived and the table is set with

a candle ready to be lit at a moment's notice. Betty is dressed in a lovely, long, silky nightgown—ocean blue with lace in all the right spots. Her nightgown is called Three Hearts of Blue. The first heart drips over her shoulders, coming to a point right between her breasts. The second heart, made of lace, wraps itself around her breast, coming to a point at her navel. Leaving a nice design circled around her nipples so they can stick out of the nightgown to be clearly seen for play and pleasure. The third heart opens in half in the private garden of Betty. Two slits come on each side of the long nightgown for easy access, surrounded with lace for the beauty of her long legs when sitting down to rub on for play. Slowly up and down.

Nel arrives as the candle is being lit, and the lights go down low. Conway Twitty's hit song *Slow Hand* plays in the background. Nel is taken away by Betty's nightgown.

BETTY: Would you like some wine, Nel?

NEL: Yes, I would, please.

BETTY: Do you like that song? It's how I like to live life: nice and slow.

He clearly knows what her body is saying to his. *Role it back to a slow roll, my boy.*

NEL: You know Conway was not the first to sing that song. The Pointer Sisters did in 1981 and Conway put a male vision to it a year later.

BETTY: His real name was Harold Jenkins and he began singing at the age of 12. Let's eat, Nel.

He was so glad to sit down because he was hard by then. Betty goes to refill his glass with wine when she notices he's hard as she places her breast in his face to pour the wine. Nel stares at her as he eats.

NEL: I've never seen such a lovely nightgown. Is it from N.Y. or California, a Hollywood stars nightgown?

BETTY: No, I made it just for me and a slow-moving night of fun. Ah, that song has a way of bringing it across really smoothly. My friend, that is how to treat a real lady.

NEL (finish eating): I have a job at eight, but I have some time to give you some of that slow hand right where it counts.

Betty gets excited by his easy touch that turns her on ever so softly.

NEL (whispers): I've got a slow grove and always wanted a lady who enjoys the easy touch.

He caresses her body all over ever so softly. He gets down and eats her out to give her pleasure before pleasing himself. After he spends the next hour rubbing her body up and down, getting Betty excited, duty calls. Nel goes out of his way to make sure she knows she is wanted and how much he loves a smooth-feeling and loving woman. She walks him to the door.

BETTY: Do you really have to go?

NEL: I wish I didn't, especially tonight, I didn't expect this lovely night at all, dear. I have to work extra like this to pay the bills, sorry.

BETTY: I understand, Nel.

As Nel walks out, he sees Jill drive by and pretends not seeing her as he goes on his way. Betty watches him leave and puts her light off, as she intended to watch him go till she couldn't see anymore. She is feeling so loved that she has someone soft and gentle in her life. All of a sudden, she sees him stop. *Oh, his work was close to here no wonder he waited to leave only at eight.* She sees him put a work belt on from the street light across the street from where he stopped. She begins to think maybe if the work doesn't last long he may stop by after to spend the night. She continues to watch from the darkness of her living room.

Chapter Five:
The Lion Lady & Telephone Man

Diane is dressed up in a tiger costume and is a paying customer of Nel's. Betty watches as the lady greets Nel at the door dressed in a tiger body suit and uses the long tail to wrap around Nel's neck and pulls him in. Betty is in total shock as she continues to watch in the darkness of her trailer.

Diane has a fantasy of someone singing *The Telephone Man* by Meri Wilson to her in its entirety. She wants it in a deep voice to turn her on when it comes to "you can have it with a ding–a ling." Nel knows how to play it shy like he's never done anything like this before, though he's been at this for years and makes good money at it.

Betty is still watching to see when Nel leaves, and her heart sinks low when she sees the lights go off and the bedroom ones go on ever so low. She's confused as he went in with his work belt on, but that doesn't last long at all. She may be soft and gentle, but she's been known to be scrappy too. She's not good at sharing what she feels is hers. She feels if you have to dress like a cat to get a guy, you're low-life trash. Nel is a soft man and deserves a woman like her. Clean, soft, gentle, good cook, everything a decent man should have. She truly knows her qualities, and to her, a man who returns that soft Conway way is Nel, and she wants him. After all, he said he was looking for that kind of a woman.

Diane is having a blast with her song of the night.

DIANE: Hey lolly lolly give it to me anyway you can. Get that ding a ling to ring it's bell all over me.

She gives him a boner pill and handcuffs him to the bed. Diane knows the timing has to be right before it kicks in, so she feels it for strength and strokes his penis to test and tease him. She rubs him between his legs like men do to tease women, getting up to the point where he is begging to do it.

NEL: Diane, get on top now.

Diane wants more of a tease when he begins to wiggle to put his hard rock in her. Just when she thinks she has pushed it far enough, she hops on, putting her nipple in his mouth.

DIANE: Suck on it, baby.

Her pleasure is fast and hard as the climax is met and she lays there collecting air in total sweat.

When things calm down, she takes the handcuffs off, and they lay there caressing each other for a high performance well done.

DIANE: Nel, can I ask you a question?

NEL: Sure, hon, anything.

DIANE: What made you ever get into this sideline hobby?

NEL: Well, I was working as a carpenter in California, and one day, this old lady asked me to put her picture up in her new home. I used the tools

I had for measurements. My own off-the-wall way of doing things.

DIANE: Now, what's that supposed to mean?

Nel begins to laugh as he strokes Diane's leg up and down.

DIANE: Now come on, you can't leave me hanging like that. We've been at this long enough for me to know how you started in this, my dear.

NEL: You're in need of a good laugh today, aren't ya!

DIANE: You bet yah, now give it up before I tie you up again.

NEL: Well, instead of running for tools for that kind of job, I use my personal stick for what is a center mark. We she says she wants it in the middle of the dresser, I just stand in front of the dress and it guides me to a perfect center point.

DIANE: Are you saying your pecker guides you to center point. Oh my, tell me more.

NEL: Well, the old lady noticed me doing it and

you know what came next.

Nel takes in the reaction on her face.

DIANE: I know that's not the end of the story. How did money-making get in this story?

NEL: She told me her friend I had worked for told her I was doing that and she felt if she caught me doing it she would have fun with it, and she did. She then told me to take an envelope titled Gigolo on the counter and leave.

DIANE: How much did she pay you?

NEL: Let's just say she paid me more for that than the work I done for her. That's when the idea came into my head. I get to have fun and be serviced with pay. Who can pass that up?

DIANE: Well, that's a turn of events. You always hear how women take advantage of men, and here you are.

NEL: Some of us got it, and I got good at it. Now, let's hit the shower before I go home and get some sleep before work tomorrow. You got me all worked up again.

Nel is still hard from the boner pill Diane gave him and gets it on in the shower again. Neither expected it, as they enjoy it to the max till they break out laughing when they are done. Nel always leaves them with some encouraging words.

NEL: So nice to have a good hard one. Text me next month's song and date, Diane.

Diane: Sure will, Nel. Your money is on the counter; grab it on your way out while I dry my hair before bed.

NEL: Thanks, darling!

Diane: Thank you, Nel.

Just then, once again, Nel sees Jill drive by. He has had enough of her and believes she is watching him to start trouble. He decides to pay her a visit in the middle of the night.

Jill wakes up sick and vomits, never leaving her home much anymore. Nel is happy not to see her drive by every time he goes on his side jobs.

Betty and Diane finally meet at the mailbox as they wait for the mailman.

BETTY: Are you the one living down the road from me who was wearing a lion costume when the maintenance man showed up?

DIANE: Why yes, it was my night for fun.

BETTY: He went there for work with his work belt on.

DIANE: Oh, he was working alright. (With a little giggle.) He was being my telephone man. You know that song, I had him play it out for me.

BETTY: What's wrong with you?

DIANE: Oh, you must be new to the games.

BETTY: What do you mean games?

DIANE: Music and dress up for servicing fun.

BETTY: What on earth are you talking about? Nel said he had to go do a job for extra pay to meet his bills.

DIANE: Yes, he did, and he was paid well.

BETTY: Lady, what are you saying?

DIANE: He charges for his services, and I pay him like everyone else he services in this trailer park.

BETTY: Are you saying service as in sex?

DIANE: Why, yes, what did you think I've been saying?

Betty is beside herself.

BETTY: He loves me and there was no paying nothing. He truly loves me.

DIANE: Oh dear, first time, right? Well, honey, first time is always free, which makes you want more and you become a client. Pay for service like the rest of us.

Betty storms away, not even waiting for her mail. As she walks to her trailer, she sees John. She looks at him red-faced and walks toward him.

BETTY: You keep your perverted sidekick away from my trailer, or I'll call the cops on you both with your sick games.

John is shaken by the look on Betty's face and what she said. He heads to the office. No one in the office has ever seen John so shaken up, and has him sit down as they give him a drink of water.

MARY: Dear John, what has happened? Did you see something you shouldn't have?

JOHN: Mary, I'm in trouble; I mean, we're in trouble, or you and Allen are.

MARY: John, calm down and let's take this piece by piece and see what we need to do. Okay!

JOHN: These ladies are blaming me for things I know nothing about and it's all Nel's fault.

John fills Mary in on what has been going on with the ladies' conversations and doesn't know what is truly going on, starting with Jill, who just moved in. He then talks about Linda, who's such an innocent old lady, never meaning any harm to anyone.

When he gets to Betty, his face turns red, gasping for air to tell Mary the rest of the stories as owners of the trailer park. Betty could only say what she was at least able to say to an old man. She has been in the trailer park now for over a year, but John feels what is going on is not good.

MARY: Don't worry, John, we'll talk to Betty tomorrow and you go home and rest up. Take the rest of the week off with pay so we can have time to get to the bottom of this without you being involved in any way. Will call you on Monday to let you know if things are settled and safe for you to return to work. Okay!

John nods his head and Mary walks him to his truck so he may leave in peace. The owners, Mary and Allen, meet in private to talk about what John has just told them.

MARY: Allen, did you ever hear of your cousin doing anything like this before?

ALLEN: No, dear, I really don't know much about his life in California before he moved here to Maine. Just that he was a hard worker doing service calls, working independently as self-employed.

MARY: I think we need to find out what his self-employment really was. Let's call Betty in and talk to her first, as she was the last one to complain and hopefully can shed some light on what's going on before we call anyone else.

Jill is still sick and it has her daughter very concerned; it's been almost a month now. Jill has survived cancer and has kidney issues, so her medical history is not great. She is getting weaker by the day and never feels safe to drive, spending most of her days sleeping. She feels her time in life is coming to an end after all she's been through.

She, of course, feels it's all part of what is going on with her past surgeries for cancer and her kidney problems that still remain. She is outside waiting for her propane tank delivery to come when her neighbor says, boy, it smells like propane in the air on this crispy cold morning.

JILL: Well, it's not mine as all is new here and I

have a detector for that in my trailer.

Jill gets her delivery and decides to go out back of her trailer to check things out. She hears a small noise and sees the delivery truck driver is just down the road. She forces herself to walk as fast as she can to reach the driver before he leaves again. She explains the noise to the driver that is coming from the tank. The driver tells her he'll check on it as soon as he is done with this customer.

DRIVER: Ma'am, I found the hoses were not put on tightly so I tightened it up for you. All should be fine now.

JILL: Oh, thank you so very much.

The driver puts in a report to his office, and they also need to have it reported to the trailer park should anyone get sick.

After the propane company tightens everything up, Jill finds in the following days that she is no longer vomiting every morning. She feels so much better, and the new hope of living life comes back to her. She wonders how this happened and not have the alarm go off. She decides to call the propane company and gets told the leak was enough to make her sick because it was by her bedroom window, but not enough for the alarm to go off. Strange thoughts enter her mind as to how and why.

Chapter Six:
Trailer Park Owners Face Reality

Mary and Allen decide Mary, being a woman, should be the one to talk to Betty alone. She calls and asks Betty if she could come to the office and help her with something. Betty knows exactly what it's about and agrees to come in the next morning. She doesn't get much sleep thinking of what she will say and how to make her points clear to what Diane also said to her. She does, however, believe the owners have no clue, but wonders if the old man John from maintenance is in on it. She has no clue there are two other complains. She feels for the safety of seniors in the park who are on social security only; she has to speak up.

The next morning, Betty gets up very tired but knows there is no backing down now. She enters the office and only Mary is there. She is very glad to see that as Mary offers her coffee and they go to a private room.

MARY: Betty, you're not in any trouble, but your remarks left John shaky and we had to give him the rest of the week off. This leads us to have to ask questions as to what happened that led you to tell John what you did.

BETTY: I think you're running a scam on seniors to rob them of their money with Nel.

MARY: No. No. No. Betty, let me make this clear: we are not running a scam in any way, and we do well with the 250 trailers in the park.

BETTY: Yes, and so is Nel at $50 an hour and $300 overnights for sexual jobs with seniors. Robbing from their limited income and that's a crime.

Mary is shocked as her shoulder droop down and pauses for a moment then gets up to get herself a drink before sitting back down and continuing to speak.

MARY: I don't know what to say at this point, but if an employee is scamming our dear seniors, we need to know about it and let the law handle it.

BETTY: I was being nice to Nel after he took an interest in my choice of song and the smell of my fine cooking. I knew he was single and offered some of my home cooking and conversation. I did not expect to be drugged and taken advantage of.

The look on Mary's face is one of shock. The words that come out of her mouth after that made it clear to Betty that the owners had no clue what was going on under their name.

MARY: Oh, Dear Lord, please tell me our poor elderly seniors are not being taken advantage of like this.

As Mary vomits in the trash can, Betty tells her of the argument she had with Diane.

BETTY: He has these old ladies dressed up according to a song that was popular back in the 70s and 80s, and he has his way with them. The first night is free, but then he charges them after that and has, at times, more than one customer a night like he did with me and Diane.

BETTY (continues): You know this trailer park can be shut down real fast, and you can go to jail for letting him take advantage of seniors like this. You do know it's against the law to be a gigolo in Maine, right? Did you do a proper background check, or is he a relative, so nothing was checked on?

MARY: You make a good point, and I'll fire him right away, but please don't blame John; he knew nothing about this. Poor old man is beyond himself, knowing he was bringing him around the trailer park.

BETTY: How long was he employed here?

MARY: We can look that up and, under this situation, tell you that.

Before Mary had a chance to answer, Betty cut her off.

BETTY: Maybe I should ask the police?

MARY: Betty, please let us handle it.

Betty stands up to leave and says on the way out.

BETTY: If I see this pervert in this park, I will call the police. You won't have a trailer park left when everyone sues you.

Betty leaves at that point. Mary calls her husband, Allen. Just the sound of her voice worries him.

ALLEN: I'll be right there before you even get the first sentence out.

As Mary hangs up the phone, she starts thinking of what story she will hear from Linda and Jill when she calls them in. She begins to talk to herself out loud before her husband gets in, never realizing he has already hung the phone up and is on his way. Cousin or not, Nel has to go and get court papers to bar him from being able to enter the park. She knows it will open them up to have to explain all the whys?

Mary was about to call their attorney when Allen walks into the office. She hangs the phone up before they answer to talk to her husband.

MARY: Nel has been scamming the seniors here in our trailer park for years.

ALLEN: How many?

MARY: I don't know, but Betty believes sometimes two a night. He told her he has to do service calls after work to pay his bills. Being a gigolo is the service calls he's making.

Allen is in total shock and red anger comes from his face and voice.

MARY (continues): Betty said she can have this trailer park closed down and we go to jail for allowing such a person work around seniors, and made sure I knew gigolos are illegal in this state that can send us to jail.

ALLEN: Call Pat to cover the office and we best go to visit the lawyer and get Nel bared fast from entering the trailer park and have nothing to do with any of our residents. I'll go in my car and call the attorney for an emergency appointment and just come when Pat gets here to cover the office.

Allen rushes out the door, not even opening it enough for his body and gets himself hit by it.

Chapter Seven:
The Fall Out

Mary and Allen meet at attorney Mr. John Fitzs' office. As they get out of their cars, they meet each other halfway and embrace each other in tears.

ALLEN: I should have checked him out like we do all employees. I'm so sorry for doing this to you. We're from a religious family. I can't believe this has happened within my own family. How? How can he have done this to us. We helped him out when he moved here from California.

MARY: Let's go see what the attorney has to say.

ALLEN: Hello, Mr. Fitzs, so glad you could see us on short notice like this.

MR. FITZS (attorney): Hello, Mary and Allen. From what I understood you have an employee who is taking advantage of seniors in your park.

ALLEN: It's worse than that; he's my cousin.

When he came from California, we hired him because he was my cousin and because of that, I never did a background check.

MR. FITZS: Oh, does he have a criminal record you weren't aware of?

ALLEN: Not that I know, oh my, you got to help us.

MR. FITZS: Tell me more. You know scamming seniors is not looked at by the courts in any form of kindness or fairness. You're talking jail time here.

ALLEN: The guy has been acting and collecting from senior as a gigolo.

Mr. Fitzs laughs and stops abruptly when he sees the look on Mary and Allen's faces.

MR. FITZS: Oh, my, this is bad.

Mary tells the attorney how their ground management supervisor came to them, speaking of angry resident remarks and the helper Nel. The poor old man was so shaken we gave him the week off with pay, of course, till we can get more information on the story.

ALLEN: I told Mary to call in the last upset lady to collect what was going on. Being a woman it would be best if I wasn't there, but I never believed a cousin of mind was doing this. We knew nothing about it. I swear to you.

MARY: I spoke to Betty, one who was last to complain to John the grounds keeper. She tells of horrible sex acts Nel has been doing with our seniors for $50 an hour or $300 a night. He claims he needs the income to pay his bills. He plays dress up with these seniors to fill their fantasies, but some are just down-to-earth rapes by drugging them and having his way with them.

MR. FITZS: First of all, I hope you fired him on the spot.

ALLEN: I need more than that; I need a protection order to stop him from entering the park and continuing this after we fire him.

Allen shakes his head and places it in his hands

in total disgrace.

ALLEN (continues): How many and what am I going to do?

Mary tells Mr. Fitzs about Betty's threat of taking the park away and sending us to jail for what Nel has done. A moment of silence as the attorney sits back in his chair, and Mary and Allen await what he is going to say next.

MR. FITZS: First, let me tell you, in California, that may be alright, but not here in Maine. You need to know the laws of a state when you move to that state. Regardless, crimes against seniors are dealt with very harshly in this state.

ALLEN: What are we talking about here? A huge fine?

MR. FITZS: You can be looking at fifteen years per person.

MARY: Dear Lord, you can be taking the rest of our lives.

MR. FITZS: That's not all. For each case you can

get that much time on probation and from 200 to 300 thousand dollars fine on each. That fine depends on failure to report that would fall on the old man John. He'd be in trouble, too, here.

MARY: But why John?

MR. FITZS: He failed to report the first incident and it would also depend on increased harm to Nel's clients, like body harm as well as mental harm, done from such an act.

ALLEN: So the law is hard on this even if we knew nothing about this.

MR.FITZS: It all falls under the Elder Justice Act that became law in 2010. All part of the Patient Protection and Affordable Care Act to protect our senior citizens. Relative or not, you're running a business and should have done that background check to protect your seniors. You do run a park for seniors and this law will be part of your case.

Mary is in total tears and Allen is pasting the floor, rubbing his chin and thinking with his head hung down.

MR FITZS: You both need to think good and hard on this one and fast. You have no time to waste and let this brew. It will only get worse if you don't act fast. First, you need to fire him today and tell him to stay out of the park, or he'll be arrested. In the meantime, I'll get a protection order to protect your seniors in the park. Are you ready to find out how many ladies will be calling you for him? Those who enjoyed the service will be calling to find out where he is.

Mary knotted.

MARY: Yes! I'll be answering the phone and taking notes of who asks.

MR.FITZS: Great, that will help us know what we're dealing with. Have any lawsuits been filed against the park that you know of?

ALLEN: Nothing has come to us yet and we don't know of any coming yet, but I'm afraid!

MR.FITZS: Be ready for that and in a court of

law, it will be hard to say if this has been going on for years that you knew nothing about this. So, have you thought of selling out at this time in your life before anything happens?

MARY: Do you think we can go to jail for not checking his background out like we do all other employees?

MR. FITZS: Yes, for sure, a point that is not in your favor. You own a senior park; don't forget that part.

ALLEN: Can we sell out quickly without anyone in the park knowing we're selling?

MR. FITZS: It's your park and you can do as you wish at any time as long as no one has or puts a lien on it.

ALLEN: He's been with us so long. I feel there are over 30 ladies; as Betty said, at times, he has two a night.

MR.FITZS: Dear Lord, what has happened to our dear seniors not only physically but mentally and financially? Those are the point a court would look at in this case and that doesn't look well for you guys at all. It's preying on seniors, no matter which way you look at it.

ALLEN: The man must be worn out by now, but he takes those pills like candy.

MR. FITZS: He'll have a heart attack at some point for that. You may be doing him a favor, putting a stop to this now.

MARY: We're looking to save ourselves from jail and that's all I care about right now.

Mr. FITZS: Okay, so are we thinking of selling right now? Ready to retire? So quietly and fast to be ahead of this?

Mary and Allen look at each other and say YES at the same time.

ALLEN: It's time to retire.

Mary and Allen stand up as Allen shakes Mr. Fitzs' hand.

Mr. FITZS: I'll handle it all for you; just lay low

till this is over. No more talking to anyone about this, and stay away as best you can if you can have someone cover for you in the office.

ALLEN: Will do, sir. Thank you so much.

Three weeks go by, and all residents get a letter in the mail they need to sign for. Betty doesn't know they all are getting one and fears she may have to move till she looks around and sees everyone is in line signing for theirs. She breathes a sigh of relief after she gets hers and hears others talking about the fact that the trailer park has been sold and they are now under new management.

THE END

Please check out some of my other books.

Toxic Fall

Paws of Fate

Splash of Love

Broken Hearts & Souls

Life of an Old Woodsman

The Torments of the Modest Secluded Farm Life

Easy & Inexpensive Holiday Classroom Crafts for Teachers

All on Amazon to buy.

About the Author

Back in 1981, I became a certified community advocate helping my community. From Tiny Todd group leader raising funds to benefit low-income kids and helping low-income families in areas that I was trained in.

In 1984, I received a certificate for my volunteer service from the University of Maine co-operative service. It was all about helping kids to learn to cook and have proper nutritional values.

I then became the treasurer of the Task Force on Human Needs and became a member of the board of directors.

Also was the vice president of the Maine Association of Independent Neighborhoods, working on pieces of legislation to help the community. As well as vice president of the American Legion Auxiliary in Lisbon Falls helping vets and raising funds.

I then spent many years doing voluntary work in schools and receiving many awards, starting with Head Start and then three different schools. Making costumes for plays, publishing the kids' personal classroom books, and fluoride treatment for one whole school weekly, I would do crafts to help what they did learn to stick a bit better.

Now, at the age of 70, I bring stories to life.